Mary E. Cox

Mary E. Cox

Within a Tradition

FOR W. H. AUDEN

WITHIN A TRADITION

Elizabeth Gerwig Shipman

THE MITRE PRESS · LONDON
52 LINCOLN'S INN FIELDS, WC2A 3NW

Printed in Gt. Britain for the Mitre Press
(Fudge & Co. Ltd.) London

CONTENTS

CONTENTS (Contd.)

THE DUKE OF WINDSOR
(From Da Vinci's Head of Christ)

Stranger than the reaches of time, fair, sweet,
Dream mirrored deep as mercy streaming bright
With spring's young ecstasy little fishes fight
Blithe as he, greet the random rose,
Song entwined where Jove, repose disposed,
Serves host at night before the supreme mystery.
And prove, white flame, like lovely pleasure, sleep.

Further knowledge, then, rewards you ours
Beyond those languors wisdom forbids all
Flesh for plundering, where the infinite casually walls
Oblivion; where bells lean like those truths
Thought grants gleaned from jeweled views
The arts proffer your radiant mind, informed,
Nor coerced from ancient faith but unique and empowered.

Now welcomed by comraderie-throngs that share,
    condoned,
(Enthrallment also divine) your prayer's unrest,
Endure as well where the splendor of your breast
Lends miracle to those griefs not forever despised,
But, assuaged, are kissed beneath their golden eyes,
Indifferent with desire as they affirm,
Confirm, the ornament of the world reborn, enthroned.

BROOK PLACE — NEW HAMPSHIRE

There where brook meets brook, streaming at widening
    angles
Over glossy rock, bubbling a million bubbles like
    champagne
In its long-stemmed glasses, and through whose
    effervescent pool
An occasional fish passes smoothly as any jet
But without sound, and lost in contemplation fixed by eyes
Also fixed as if in death, I pause, looking for the word
    I want,
The words I want, the lines, stanzas, the completed
    verse,
As might have Thomas Wolfe or Dylan Thomas, those
    giants who live now
In mammoth, snowy cloud-forms, engaging the sky in
    creation for my sake.
These, and can I forget Whitman, oh poet of the human
    god and circumstance!
But I find that this proof of the ecstasy in nature
Is only a reminder of its strength, not the answer to my
    problem,
Great yet infinitely small, craven yet proud, bent on
    instruction,
So that it is possible that I am jealous of the evidence
    life gives of renewal —
Flowing onward, renegade, in an energetic cognition
    that has nothing to do
With words as I desire to use them, deliberate jewels,
    meaningful as equated number!
Here I return to my private study, my table made of
    glass so often visited,
There to indulge in the search for exact expression and
    its virile execution.
Oh finite soul of the world, you are lost in the expanses
    of a mightier identity,
Yet whirl swiftly within sight of one of its suns and
    blinded, owe no gift to any man.

FOR THE MODERN POET

A glittering web of sheerest silk,
On Poet of fact and calm despair,
Your subtle textures, mild as milk,
Nobly difficult visions dare
Of familiar, starry skies like ours
Where arrogant gods and Christians walk,
Chaotic, random earth empowering,
Its puzzled hearts to heal and lock,
In transformation won exacting
As echoes to a source reacting.

IT'S A BATTLE

Cock white
Takes the fight;
(Spurs as sharp as bankers' bids.)

Wits keen
Claim the scene;
(A nation's race and place at stake.)

Furthest shore
Remains at war;
(Where blood is spilled like falling stars.)

But Chair bold
Holds the fold;
(Disavowing world dominion.)

Shall Communist horde
Wield strong the sword?
(Extensive lands of this belief.)

Although billions dared
Can well be spared;
(Planes and ships cost something, too.)

Cock white
continues fight;
(Spurs as heavy as the price on gold.)

MY AUNT

The rain streams down; the thunder roars;
Jagged lightning trims the sky;
The trees, like dancers, curve and sway;
The wind, a ghostling, seems to sigh;
And from the porch I look into
A room that's bright with warm, soft light;
Absorbed, she sits, white scarf around
Her shoulders like the queen of night;
Her downward glance and rapid pen
Mark her writing letters there,
And although she's unaware of me,
I know I her attention share.

CONSERVATIVE

Are there depths to light,
And heights, likewise?
We'll take the right
While the multitude sighs.

Are there words to speak,
Commands to give?
Christ was meek;
Our faith will live.

Are there lips to kiss,
Are there arms to hold,
While the hours list,
And the moon is bold?

There is all of this,
And more besides;
Just now we'll insist
That your patience abides,

That a strength of steel
Possess your will,
That you may not feel
That law is nil,

Since poets and horses,
Starry equations,
Regard other sources
As so many evasions!

ARISTOCRAT

I'll try to succeed in convincing you
That equality simply doesn't exist,
That nature prefers a stricter view,
Poverty firmly to resist;
Nor do I speak of your wallet or bank,
Nor of your physiognomy,
Nor necessarily of your rank,
Or of your skill at trigonometry;
But of an energy, deep and controlled,
That trusts in forgiveness and perfect love,
Yet commands a view-point, calm yet bold,
When asked to concede to a power above.

JUSTICE
(A Portrait)

A skin of ivory you cannot forget,
Eyes like thought's dark jewels,
These reflect a strange regret,
Deep in their drowning, brilliant pools;

A mouth that's cut like a whip's thin length,
Echoes love's command:
That law and order require of strength
A peaceful day in a rebel land.

THE AMERICAN PEOPLE SAY: "TELL US!"

Tell us again of that resignation
There in the underground of the Berlin Chancellery;
Tell us of the gun, the bride of a day,
And the immortal self-sacrifice, the burning dust;
The disruption and ruin of the Aryan mother,
The wanton destruction of our highest reason.

Remind us of those powerful, Slavic armies
That raged against the rightful friend;
Of the child onrushing from the west,
Adding its weight to the betrayal
Of a virile cause,
Hated and feared by an elegant demagogue.

Did Christ live again?
And did we forsake Him?
Sick and haggling women take the picnic grounds,
A tribe grieving for want of homeland and love —
But the cry is never ending,
And the response cursory, filled with reserve.

Is the shame, then, to live? Even at war?
Battling a principled people for its own land,
We assert ourselves; but not in the name of race;
Of this we are afraid —
Our own being confused, dissatisfied even with luxury;
The unhappiest of it misled, and beginning to know it.

FOUR SONNETS

My Mommy

I think my daddy loves me more than mommy,
Although she kisses me with gentlest care,
Since when I'm with him everything is balmy,
And all the world is mine with him to share;
He always takes an interest in my toys,
And asks me which of these I like the best,
While mommy says that I make too much noise,
That I should go away to give her rest.
And yet I know my mommy's always right,
Since daddy also says that this is so;
And when she sits beside my bed at night,
Around her hair there seems to be a glow
Of sunlight just as if the dark were morning,
While sleep comes down without a single warning.

Solved

Peace possess the world, the day has come
When no time but the present shall prevail,
Forgiveness having added up her sum
Of wrongs and sent them ocean-ward to sail.
And there they sink beyond the sight of man,
Deep rest upon the welcoming, golden sands
Where mermaids sometimes visit but to ban
All thought of them or of their native lands!
And there they form a club discussing how
They might again ascend to earthly power,
But argue so among themselves that now
There's nothing much but sea-weed left to glower;
While from the rocks the friendly sirens sing
That fear is dead and gulls are on the wing!

An Accord

Beyond the crystal reaches of all time,
Among the stars' and planets' glittering spheres,
Within the depths of space whose ordered rhyme
Sings of neither joy nor passion's tears,
A part of us, invisible but sure,
Is perfectly aware of future being,
And knows that since it lives it must endure
A past that's fraught with mundane earth's dull seeing;
It seems to glance an infinite distance down,
To predicate a glory even there
Where feathered angels welcome with a frown
The sinner, too, although his heart is bare
Of all but hope for heaven with its gold,
Where even puling child may not grow old.

Reward

The trees are bare of leaves; all heaven is gray;
The grass that once was green has turned to brown;
The little squirrels, half starved, now seem to say:
"For him who feeds us there will be a crown
Of thanks much brighter than the iciest diamonds,
Of sapphires like the mid-December sky,
Of emeralds shining like those winter ponds
That hide within the woods from passers-by.
His lips shall be like holly berries, red,
His cheeks the color of the sun-set snow,
His gift remembered as we go to bed
Within the oak's trunk, warm and safe from woe,
As there we pray that he may live forever,
Protected by his great and good endeavor.

A FRIEND

In the dining room of an empty bar,
We stopped for a sandwich and drink;
Our nerves were frayed and our moods were far
From their usual, rosy pink,
When out from behind a chair there walked
A pregnant, Persian cat,
With heavy carriage and head that talked
Of a breeding very high hat.
She looked at me, alone, with eyes
Of heavenly, azure blue,
Then made her way to my surprise
Directly to me, too,
As if to say: "I know you're right
And a friend of mine so tell
Them, if you're getting ready to fight,
That you're not feeling well."
I petted her and said: "How pretty,
I'll take your good advice!"
With that, this partial, plume-tailed kitty,
(My soul forever enticed)
Disappeared from out of that shadowy room,
Nor seen by me again;
But I'll think of her by the light of the moon,
And whenever I take up my pen.

MOZART

Beneath the high-grown, azure sky — we lie —
Roses bloom within June's breast — at rest —
Lift upward fragrant heads for joy — Le Roi —
Then sleep within her misty veils — pale sails —
Brides lovely borne by day's great sun — one —
Now arched moon's master, flaming round —
       to ground —
And delicate there as passion's grace — like lace —
Where larks praise loud his virile face — sweet race!

BEETHOVEN

Dwarfed droning doom,
Drums crawl domed heaven,
Roar deliberate anguish
In downward-falling, fervid song,
Sustained by the giant's will
Prophetic trumpets herald truth,
Deaf calling home those arid fires
That rage beyond the tomb's entrance
Where genius pledges power's dream,
Reborn articulate.

DEBUSSEY

Usual as a great-winged bird dismayed at finding itself
Stalked to perspective single-eyed as the cruel face of
    depravity,
He remarks dual mirrors leaden beneath the ebony of
    her hair,
Webbed to the moon maid's stare at noon, and,
    enraged by desire,
Ensnares her within his breast where he ravishes her;
    ravaged,
Her mouth curves music harsh as fire rising suppliant-
    pale
Upward from the sweet of straw for the rebirth of reason
That thighs may hold him mild as skies beguiled by
    builded white.

WERE I

Oh were I to write like the poet, Ginsberg,
Subtly and divinely,
Of rebellion and of mankind's strength,
Gently yet never supinely,
I'd make a plea for a far-flung vision,
Including the Whitman Sea,
Where persons of every persuasion could meet
To enjoy themselves at tea.

Oh were I to write like the poetess, Moore,
Difficult and precious,
Yet forbidding the general public's ear
For fear that it refreshes,
I'd enclose myself in a stony tomb,
And there compose a song
That precluded a desperate, final love,
And wait for it, yes, long.

Oh were I to write like the poet, Auden,
Whose monologues never lag,
Nor lack allusions to merry England,
That country with brilliant flag,
I'd return to Shakespeare's jewel-like sonnets,
Take them to my heart,
And prove that these I could easily out-dream
By making a brand new start!

Oh were I to write like a poet at all,
I'd affirm the poets' right
To claim and prefer an original view
Of the universe most bright;
Nor bother with capital letters, gross,
Or rhyme, of course, confining,
But agree that free verse is the only one left
To argue my art is refining.

BUSINESS MAN
(For Paul)

Like an unexpected chord in an already exciting and
  cacophonous symphony,
I find you sitting behind your desk
As if the splendours of a blue and black and white-
  checked blue-jay
Flattered the branches of an otherwise winter tree,
There engaged in accounts, self absorbed
As the heart of a pink-petaled, late, June rose.
And I know once again the meaning of my love for you:
It is as though my father and my husband and my
  brother
Were captured in your abstracted being,
Freeing me of each discipline, yet celebrating all,
And sharing in an approval, never expressed,
But felt as if you had embraced me and shaken my hand.

PATIENT HIPPIE

I thought I'd call him a hopping clown
With his hair worn almost down to the ground;
I wrote a verse to that effect,
But stopped a moment then to reflect
That his music and dance turn the world around,
That this Rock 'n Folk and T.V. renown
Keep us all crying yet smiling, too,
Since without them we'd be in a sillier stew!

ROSES
(For Gertrude Stein)

Roses, the ashes of roses, roses, pink roses;
A mouth of silk and the dawn's first dew-drops
On roses, roses, pink roses, the ashes of roses;
Where a fire burned slow as reason's soul
Against a mouth of pink roses, the symbol of roses;
Where a fire closely pressed with love's desire
And the glow of roses for roses and roses, pink roses,
Burned like pink roses, the essence of roses.

YOUNG NEGRESS

Brown as the moistened, fragrant earth,
Pink-lipped as the full-blown rose,
Strong as the chosen one from birth,
Slow to acknowledge, quick to suppose,
Her senses keen as a knife's steel blade,
Her brow of bony power made,
Her eyes the brilliant, midnight stars,
Her breast with its curving tips sweet bars
All reason for arrogance, prejudice, tight,
And argues for love, both deep and bedight.

WARNING

I'm the devil's spawn;
Just look me over;
In your face I'll yawn
Since I live in clover.
Ask me a question:
I'll answer: "No!"
Give a suggestion,
I'll deal you a blow.
I'm not afraid
Of any you,
And I'll take a blade
Of steely blue,
And cut you up
Into bloody pieces;
You nasty pup,
And all your nieces!

RHYME

Subtler wits than mine have said that love is quite
    assuming,
And to occupations turn, dull other thoughts resuming;
But like birds and sunlight, swift, I find it most
    presuming
To think that it can anything be but pleasure all
    consuming.
And yet I live for reason, alone, idea's world attempting,
Evasion's dross and violent deed, at will, entirely
    exempting,
But find myself the smiles of friends and flowers sweet
    preempting,
But not, by choice, with flattery, for worldly view
    relenting.

GOOD MORNING

White and gold chrysanthemums
Glow from the library table;
Beautiful, their glory sums
Nature's living fable,
That death and grief can matter not,
Nor evil hold its sway,
When form and loveliness are caught
To charm a scholar's day!

THE BEGINNERS' CHESS

The King moves one square anywhere,
And forces all in each direction;
The Queen, from every distance, fair,
Travels and conquers with predilection;
The Rook, in level or vertical form,
Demands his noble, clear-eyed right;
And the Bishop, within an angular norm,
Keeps the board within his sight.
The Knight rides two, jumps cross-wise, one,
From red to black or opposite fending;
While the Pawns open double, then singles, run,
And at corners war for the field, unending.
But when from a threat the King can't move,
The game is won by the cleverer man;
Nor can the other, mated, prove,
How daring his gains nor how bold his plan.

A CHESS PIECE

I looked at her and thought to myself:
"She certainly resembles a pawn;
The only one of the pieces here
That doesn't make me yawn.
You could play a game with her and win;
She's strong and sturdy and wise;
Perhaps since her part is a humble one,
No treachery lies in her eyes."

JACKPOT

A silver horse, a silver moon,
A silver butterfly,
Silver rain and a silver tune,
The silver, twilit sky,
Silver winds and silver wheels,
Silver shoes and gown,
Silver fans and silver keels,
A silver, mist-borne town,
Silver spoons and silver forks,
A silver tea-set, gleaming,
Silver dunes and silver corks,
Silver finds us dreaming
OF,
A golden chain, a golden ring,
A golden mop of hair,
A golden verse, a golden wing,
A golden trumpet's blare,
A golden sun, a golden hope,
Some golden coins, as well,
A golden thought, a golden rope,
Golden stars that tell
Of a golden life in after death,
And a golden bell to speak
Of a golden rule's sweet, golden breath,
And golden angels, meek.

RUTH

Like a child whose age is three,
She beckons to the heart of me,
And seems to walk as if the world
Before her lovely eyes were curled —
Its vice and wrong, all silly things,
Its voice, a joy that shouts and sings,
Its gold, a locket, 'round her throat,
Its gift, the birdling's flight and note;
Her speech is grave, low-toned and sweet;
Her smile will every stranger meet
To send him on his lonely way,
As if an angel blessed his day.

PASTEL

Glorious sphere, oh lightning orb,
Your living, sentient things are heightened
To shapes and forms with joy now filled;
The bluest domes of far-flung skies
Remain your spacious, radiant home,
And welcome you each fragile morning,
Bid farewell as evening falls.
The emerald green of trees and grasses,
The glossy gold of ripening wheat,
The mighty seas of gray and ermine,
Roar your mastery, sing your song,
While white and pink and lavender flowers
Bespeak from fragrant earth your praise,
And human love still adds its knowledge,
Sweet and strong to meet your gaze.

TO THE NOVEMBER SUN

Enamoured, I watch you
Throughout the day
At every possible hour,
Oh omnipotent and spherical sun,
Sparkling through the forest's branches
In golden, crystalline dew;
Now rising steadily westward,
A trillion moons strong,
Above an otherwise gray,
Prehistoric, murky landscape.
I see this landscape, too,
In its elephantine colors
Soft as kittens' paws;
The branches of the oaks
(Bronze now hung)
Black and dark as midnight
Glowing against the loyal day-earth
That upholds them.

At noon,
Glancing upward,
I falter, blinded by your glittering stare,
Proud yet humbled,
And praise you before all else and others,
You, the source of my life,
My continued well-being;
Father and mother, god and goddess,
One and indomitable
Without whom no life is possible
Or love or grief or even blessed death.
Sun, sunlight, the night descends
Bathing your glory
In starry oblivion.
And I wait for you another dawn
In my infinitude of smallness.

THE NEEDLER

The struggles, the games are about to begin,
The pieces put in their proper places;
Tell us, then, where have you been?
What are your names, we know your faces.
What side do you take in the Arab war,
Is Viet Nam a topic with you,
Are all men equal down to the core
Or do you take the more personal view?

CONSEQUENCE

Violence knows beginning and end,
But little of the middle,
A fury imposed, a fever spent
Upon a hateful riddle.
Sometimes its reason lies beneath
A sense of the unequal,
But usually it does not care
What wrong may be its sequel.

ERRANT

Among the trees the summer wind
Turns their leaves to bells
That sing a song of love well lost
To death's swift, cooling dells;
Plays as well with the burning sun,
Reflects him upside down,
As you can see by the shadows there,
Dancing on the ground.

RECOMPENSE

The only reason death is feared
Is that it marks a change
From dress of flesh so long endeared
By habit's pleasant range.
Yet now as from the bone it slips,
Gently as a feather,
A vision, clear, the future grips,
That welcomes every weather.

SHIRLEY

She's sweet as a rose;
Looks like a Persian kitten,
Stands pat on her little feet,
Clasps the stone ledge with her little hands
And sings with the birds.

EARLY SPRING

This is for you — all of it:
A curving, rainy road, gray, leading to the highway
On whose one side familiar buildings stand,
(Buildings we both know well)
On the other, a brown lawn from which the as yet leafless
    oak and maple grow.

This is for you — all of it:
A heart that beats for you — no other,
(Knowing well the conditions)
But that finds in every casual object or gesture
An image and reminder of your strength and grace.

This is for you — all of it:
In remembrance, a black, sweet, steaming coffee,
A cigarette whose smoke wreaths around my dreams
    of you,
Here where you so often stood
Exchanging the time of day, (the amenities of hopeless
    love) with me.

This is for you — all of it:
Grass will turn green, trees their blossoming buds soon
    show,
And skies as blue as kittens' eyes and violets
Must waken then again (this deepest of all affections)
Dormant where the winter wind still blows.

A VIEW

A patio, a fence, a stretch of grass and a right-swung
    road,
Some trees that line that curving road, some day-
    parked, usual cars,
Combine to form a landscape with an iridescent glow,
Across whose sloping level, figures amble to and fro.
Today this slight activity is fixed before my eyes,
Where shadow and the sun's soft light play a
    predestined game,
Where birds, like accents, ebony-black, march with
    proud delight,
And all the crystal world's at peace within their perfect
    sight.

GREETINGS

After a long time, you are present again, standing there,
Swarthy-skinned and tall, absorbed, giving the
     impression of leprous white;
And there is nothing more to venture but a vague:
     "Hello, remegade, I'm fine, just fine.
I'll keep my cruel, unspoken remonstrance for a
     non-existent other time."
You are complaisant; I'd say you almost smiled there
     where you casually waited
For me, somehow, and yet, not at all; not wanting nor
     giving recognition, even,
But confident of your own delightful existence; then
     slouched like an old man
With an uneasy conscience and much more to account
     for, out into an open-doored, red sedan.

RAIN TODAY

Heavy, soft, oh silver rain,
Reflected in the leaf's dull gleaming,
Reflected in the pavements lain
Like mirrors' surface, crystal seeming,
You fall alike on man and beast,
Cooling sweet the bird's parched throat,
Cooling, then, those hearts that least
Upon your healing powers dote;
And yet within their secret souls,
Adore your harvest's teeming wealth,
Adore your fragrant earth's green stoles,
And walk in you, refreshed, for health.

AND RAIN TODAY

A shimmering veil of clover's petals
Drops from the cloudy sky,
And on the earth its fragrance settles
Sweet as a lambling's cry.
And its silver silk, its crystal mesh,
Soft as mercy's eyes,
Cool our sun-warmed, sun-tanned flesh
As swiftly as umbrellas rise.

FROM MY GRAVE

As the flesh slips from my bones,
All I've read in ponderous tomes,
Will haunt me like the glimmering day,
Angels laughing, soft at play:
But somewhere else, not close beside me —
I prefer nice worms at tea;
Whirling spheres my hopes resolving,
Nor future life at length involving.

MY LAST DUCHESS
(From a Poem of the same name by Robert Browning)

Does your portrait hang there still,
Above the ancient, heavy stairway,
Carved in walnut, gleaming dark?
Yes, there you stand, so delicate, gay.
Of palest pink your lips are shaded,
Your eyes are deep as drowning pools,
Like the heart your chin is curved,
Your forehead of that type that rules.
But who can speak, then, of your contours?
Voluptuous, for love's strength borne,
As the dove's that follows Venus,
This picture's proofs the walls adorn,
Where, cursed, you knew a husband's sword,
Saw the blood fall from your breast,
Realized his jealous will
That gave him neither peace nor rest.
And through the spectre's words he speaks:
"I envied her her faintest smile;
I loved her with a madness, mortal,
And yet she did all things beguile.
The servants gave her personal pleasure;
The trees, the grass, the flowers, small,
Commanded, then, her young delight.
She glanced approval at them all.
And so within the candlelight
Of our bedroom great with hope and gloom,
I reached in truth her throbbing being,
Sent her to her early doom.
I could no longer live nor breathe,
Her passion with each creature sharing;
Now blest she hangs upon my wall,
Beyond all joy or possible caring."

BLACK SWAN

That love at once my veins should fill with overflowing
    sweet,
Immaculate sharing by you alone nor secret held,
Honor leans led fledgling young above its sacred deep,
And wakened shares a promise bright where sorrow
    dwells.

For wage the antique serpent's guile that bears the
    heart's proud ruin
From earth's reined weight empowered still and living
    borne,
Exactly where the rose invites the radiance of the moon,
That lovely light in heaven's reaches, star adorned.

But where your eyes reflect that sphere no tears quench
    dry of fire,
A various season veils its poles with vigorous dream,
As knives reward with raging crimson, justice finally sired,
And flags unfurled this passion prove, by truth
    redeemed.

WHITE SWAN

Lilies of the valley bend far down beneath the naked sky,
Lean as great as iron-clothed bells nor half so shy,
Their waxen flesh quite white as death, remarks the
    day we bid farewell,
And pointed-edged denies response, now sundered—,
    dancing.
Sweet the sound, the echo sounding, bounding where
    the grasses curve.

Deepest pools drown far-thrown stones nor ever seen
    thereafter known,
But never then forgotten, either, heart-like, close,
And throb as music tries its bonds against itself in
    proud restraint,
The universal word of grace, resolved in silence.
Deaf the answer, constant sounding, bounded where
    the grasses curve.

QUESTION

Is love child's play?
A laughing word,
A tear, you say.
A blushing smile,
An optical ray,
A sleepless night,
A heavenly day,
A song to sing,
A verse that's gay;
Moot question, yours,
Now yes, now nay.

A FAIRLY GENERAL VIEW

I'm soft as an egg inside its shell,
I witness wrong as well as right;
Compromise sees me down in hell,
And I'm kept busy sitting tight.
The murderer has his way with me,
The rebel sets my towns on fire,
Never mind this time it's Kennedy;
Ask why he did it, they'll say you conspire.
I have some ideas of good and bad,
But I'm rich so everything seems the same;
And if you think this life is sad,
I'll tell you at least it isn't tame.
Excitement I look for, that's what I want;
A sex crime, a dope fiend, a lawyer's fraud,
A plane crash, a robbery, flood lands, gaunt,
But the sport page I tell you's the work of God.

DREAM OF A CONCENTRATION CAMP

Fixed in fields of sullen sloth, I lay in terror's dream
    last night;
Straps hung from a ceiling, low, of red and gleaming,
    upcurved leather,
Bawdy, beckoned me to come and try their haunted,
    empty tether.
But restrained by chilled yet dull reluctance, a rancid
    and unearthly light,
This I could not do nor turn from pitiful, destined,
    victim's plight.

First I had on rocks run balanced; these flat and slimed
    with salty spray;
My grandmother, masked, and close behind, had
    disappeared from me together
With hope for freedom's choice, a train to catch, a
    balmy, silly weather;
And at my feet like lice there lay some soaking bread-
    crumbs, swollen splayed;
With them, proof that men had planned in hate this
    desolated play.

Now within my brain there entered conviction I was
    hopelessly lost
Beyond my reason or my strength to find my innocent
    way again,
And maddened by resistance and a desperate search
    for mercy, then,
I wakened from unconscious tension, back my blanket
    kicked and tossed,
Lit a cigarette to find myself in bed like melting frost.

MARY

Protest no more, my delicate flower,
A knife requites your petals, shy,
As Mary's eyes there in her bower,
Silver blue and ceilinged high.
Beneath her feet the grasses grow,
Mild as silken, downy feather,
While within her arms a baby's glow
Makes sweet the earth's unseemly weather !

THE BLACK RING
for R.F.K.

My tears fall on its smooth, black surface,
    Death, its import, of one so fair,
Angels envied his earth-born grace,
    Snowy-smiling, tawny-haired;
And brave to echo Lincoln's plea
    That the negro live in freedom earned,
This at a time when that turbulent sea
    Rioted wild and the cities burned.
Perhaps discretion was not for him;
    Perhaps the Arab lands he dared;
And yet we believe that a vision, undimmed,
    A common distrust and hatred bared.
A warning should have come his way,
    Since importance was his in the first degree,
To teach him that race is a problem made
    For Christ in His Tomb on bended knee.
A shrug and a bow, an evasive word,
    These for his life a trade can assume,
Now that he's gone like the summer bird
    In winter, to his early doom.

SALUTE TO THE LAW

Where?
In his grave.
Why?
As assassin's bullet.
At the desks
Thin-lipped men sat,
Eyes like steel,
Ascertaining on paper
That that bullet
Killed
A nation's prospective chief,
Its pride and joy.

There,
Sick with ambition,
A lawyer
Planned clemency.
Ornate his abode,
Fixed
With the trappings
Of the exonerated,
Freed as a result
Of his rationalizations.
This time
He failed.

PATRICIA

Through a veil of tears
I see your face
As the rain-drops fall,
And winter nears,
Its pearly white.
Like an angel's soul,
Gleams in the dark
As the moon's pale light.
Your eyes of the sea,
Your tender mouth,
Your soft, brown hair,
Sweet comfort me,
And your spoken words,
From love's mild lips,
Strengthen my heart
As a singing bird's.

MR. GENIUS

Tall, slender, stooped,
You look as though the world had duped you.

Remote, reserved, complete,
Perhaps, for spite, the fates defeat you.

Abstract, assured, benign,
Close study then designs to blind you.

Since, welcoming, weeping, laughing,
My thoughts at sight of you are baffling.

A NOVEMBER AFTERNOON

Pink roses and daisies seven feet under —
    I wonder
What the world is coming to.
    Blue
Skies above us and brown earth below —
    Glow
Like jewels in a soft, velvet box.
    Locks
On the doors and snow at the panes —
    Death refrains
From her usual song.
    Long
Time ago, I loved you as now —
    How?
As the moon loves the sun —
    Oh Glorious One!

SAFE

She holds a kitten in her arms,
And he's contented and happy to be,
Safe from all that loudly alarms,
A barking dog or you or me.

KEEP OFF

A fence was made for beauty's sake,
And forbids the marauder's bold intrusion;
A lawn, some trees, a smooth, blue lake,
Are reasons enough for enforced seclusion.

GRASSY LAWN

Laden with sunlight and shadows, tall,
Bound by a hedge of darker green,
Nor burdened by house or stony wall,
You constitute a most restful scene.

RARE SIGHT

A lady in pink requites the scene
With dainty step and parasol,
And in this time of legs' bare lean,
Manages quite to embarrass us all!

NORTH VIET NAM TO SOUTH VIET NAM

Oh did you cast your pearls
    Bedight,
Before the pink-skinned, warring swine?

And did you love his curls
    Like light,
More than your own, jet-black kind?

And did you see the river swirl,
    A sight
That warned you it would find

Little, slant-eyed, golden girls
    Who fight
The family ties that bind?

Within those depths that stream and whirl
    At heights
There lives the new moon's rind;

Since there she did herself then hurl
    At night,
Fate's proof that love's divine.

FRIENDSHIP

Pure as the winter's driving snow,
Strong as the summer's rising sun,
Swift to your heart does my heart go,
Swift to your arms do I then run.

Rare as the words of truth said slowly,
Deep as the ocean's farthest blue,
Now do I claim your friendship wholly,
Now shall I dwell with your love anew.

Sweet as the rose, your delicate smile,
Keen as the lightning's fire, your glance,
These of my soul have freed all guile,
These my life and death enhance.

THESE DAUGHTERS

Contrary says she won't, she will,
She makes us all quite tired and ill;
Difficult says I'm scared, I can't,
She hears her mother rave and rant;
Foolish says I'm right, not wrong,
We listen to her much too long;
While impudent a cookie takes,
Then says she doesn't much like cakes.
Of these four types I like the best,
The one that's different from the rest.

RESIGNATION

How quickly does the hour's mood
Change from joy to grief's dull sense,
And with it every lasting good,
From sweet become obeisance,
Fixed to clocks and darkening skies,
Doors that close, friends that frown;
When at last shall we be able
These to judge, yes, force them down?

But would we hope for constant pleasure?
Birds that sing without a rest,
A sun that shines through every cloud,
And never puts belief to test?
Oh no, we think not, even so;
The way things are is usually best;
But let us without doubt soon know
That mostly always life is blest.

AGAIN

Daring the jagged coast,
At odds with a starless sky,
Dream, then, of the sun
Rising at midnight.
Relinquish the fight,
Fall back on the beach,
Sink into it
And, if necessary,
Grovel there in the sand.
No-one cares,
No agony endures,
Sleep comes at last,
And with it —
Revelation!

FOR MARTIN LUTHER KING

Frequent the roses, petaled soft,
Fragrant their delicate bloom;
Mighty the oak trees, held aloft
Within the sky's big room.
Swiftly the birds fly, hard to approach,
No matter how I try;
But where is my loved one, lain in a coach
That passed indifferently by.

Warm are the tears on wrinkled cheek,
Deep the sobbing I hear;
Shall we, then, forever seek
Our loved ones once so near?
Frequent the roses, petaled soft,
Fragrant their delicate bloom;
Mighty the oak trees, held aloft
Within that empty room.

A DELIBERATION

For Michael Zukoff

At the center of a small, tall wood
    they cluster like a fountain of blood and rise,
These red ramblers, empty of fragrance
    and heavy with sharp-edged, oval leaves;
Their cone-thornéd stems treasured
    swollen and stark as the Christ's cruel eyes,
Tangling one with the other in passionate profusion
    beneath the sky's far eaves.

And from them I cut enough
    to make a generous bouquet for a gardner friend
Of Russian descent, charming and intransigent,
    since I desire to offer him
A gift whose semblance to certainty, long accustomed
    to conquest and death, mend; in token, blend;
There beneath the sun's impartial nor impatient
    gold and crimson, Parisian rim.

FOR THE EMPEROR MARCUS AURELIUS, STOIC

Your eyes are like jewels,
    Pools
Now deep as midnight,
    The sun's light
Praising death
    And autumn's perfumed breath.
They are the ashes of roses
    Where repose
The symbols of desire,
    Inspiring
The soul's rebirth,
    In dearth
Of belief, to the nourishing of intellect
    And reflection.
How repay their gift?
    Oh swift
Our beings to honor,
    To don
Like gold their speech —
    Nor reach
Remote for stranger love.
    A dove
Spreads pearl-white wings,
    Brings
Peace to those despairing hearts
    That courage parts
From hope and pain, these one,
    Denied in truth by none.

EARLY

I walk through the familiar woods dressed in white,
With green suede, black strapped, gold-buckled
    slippers,
Carrying two bags, one of dark red leather,
And one of pink flowers, smoking a cigarette:
Chesterfields.

The walk curves south-west through the woods
In the direction that I want to go,
And is made of unevenly cut blocks of stone
Of slate-blue and gray,
So that I have to watch my step
In order not to turn my ankles,
Although the heels of my shoes are square and flat.

And through these woods, the oak and maple and pine
Rise above the green-sward
On which occasional grackles of svelte ebony,
Cerise, blue and emerald at necks and heads,
Leaden-eyed and slow, lift dusky, shrunken claws;
Peck for seeds or fly with powerful wings
Into a waiting oak or pine;
Or skim, shadowing the grass.
Suddenly a tall, young negro strides toward me.
Open collared and bronze-satin skinned and passes
    quickly by.

The mist is heavy among the trees' branches and ascends
Through the grass like a Chopin Nocturne interpreted
    by Marguerite Long,
Or the instrumental music to Parsifal and simulating
    these,
Opens vistas to fresh yet gold-intricate and involved
    worlds
Exquisitely wrought, where lovely women and prophets
    walk;
Where violins by Eliot sing,
Accompanied by harps and drums, the cymbol and the
    Word.

Here, a young starling, horizontal as a chess-board,
        reminds me
That metaphors are necessarily in agreement, one with
        the other,
And a sparrow, one, two, three, four, five, six sparrows!
Sparkling earthen, black and gray, far upward,
        skyward!
Affirm her rectitude.

I do not laugh with joy but say farewell,
FOR THE TIME BEING (Auden's) loving birds the
        best of all,
While a stranger, but perhaps a blue-jay — I am not
        certain which —
Pours forth drowning, cut, swooning sapphires from a
        curving branch that sways
Through the morning clouds,
Promising azure skies and a BRILLIANT SUN.

LIKE ME

Like the spider spinning her web
Of shining silk, iridescent gray,
Back and forth from tree to post,
Throughout the live-long, busy day,
Or purling there from ceiling's rim,
Beyond destructive house-wife's reach,
I write small words for your delight,
Hoping that they will also teach
That life is like the whirling sun,
And seen from any, little distance,
Includes the great and small, alike —
The spider and her web, for instance.

BY TRUTH SPENT

Can we count on our fingers the time gone by,
Is a century as much as a second?
Are the winds of the numberless winters gone by,
With the roses and lilacs, as well, to be reckoned?

Do lovers' words express a truth,
That lives beyond the sky and sea,
Shall there be any echo of any truth,
Or only a silence, shockingly free?

Does death account for lives well spent,
Are there many others we should remember?
What difference when all is ventured and spent,
Though Christ was born in the month of December?

Shall He absolve us of our sin,
And shall we be pardoned our tiresome lot?
Who is to say we are guilty of sin,
When so little we want can be borrowed or bought?

QUEST

Sing, oh whispering, silver, summer wind
Among the grasses' pliant, knife-like blades,
Like water streaming breasted cool and finned
By mighty fish and roaring, swift decades;
And there within your secret, wandering soul,
Hold these my passionate words for mankind's sake,
That you may carry safe to furthest goal
A thirst for freedom's birth as yet unslaked.

HOME

A curving branch and brilliant grass, a heavy atmosphere
    and sky,
Take me home to my aunt's house and a silver tea-set,
    engraved and high;
There we'll sip our lemony drink, exchange a sweet
    and familiar word,
And with the swift and cooling rain, call the world's
    concerns absurd.

THE ATOM

Tinier than a dew-drop,
Blond as the motes of the sun,
There at the rainbow's top,
Venus, having fun,
With a gleaming emerald sea,
Tossed some feathery foam
Direct and straight at me,
And then a golden comb.

I tried my level best
To catch this proof of love,
But lost it in the crest
Of a sea-gull's wing above;
Gray and white he flew
Aslant his homing waters,
As though her gift, he knew,
Was meant for earthly daughters!

A DREAM AND A PROPHECY

Dreaming of death that is sure to come,
The release of our flesh and soul,
The becoming as one with the universe;
Hark! a bell does toll!
Far from the earth yet a part of it,
Held in its close embrace,
Warm as against our mother's breast;
Sweet as the blood of race —
Shall there be further breath to take,
The spirit find itself free
To share in distant, sapphire space?
Tell us! we feel it to be!
Nor further knowledge of grief and pain
Mourning this world's short span,
But certainty of rebirth alone;
This is the fate of man!